WORLD OF RACING

KART RACING

By Sylvia Wilkinson

Consultants: John Morton
Mike Manning
Doug Stokes

CHILDRENS PRESS ®
CHICAGO

Sprint karts race at Las Vegas "Tropicana Kart Prix"

Photo Credits

Doug Stokes: 2, 12, 15 (2 photos), 19, 33, 40 (top)

John Duke Photo: 16

Photo Courtesy of Ruth Ingels: 13

Mack Photos: 4 (2 photos), 8 (2 photos), 9, 11, 21, 24

John Morton: 14

Mike Manning Karting: 17

Joey Cavaglieri: 22, 23 (left)

Kathy Eddy: Front cover (top photo), back cover (both photos), 23 (right), 30, 40 (bottom), 42

David L. Williams: 27, 28, 34, 35 (2 photos), 36 (2 photos)

Kelly Arrison: 31

Photo by Spider: 7

Mike Edick: Front cover (bottom photo)

Robert Harmeyer, Jr.: 38, 39

Library of Congress Cataloging-in-Publication Data
Wilkinson, Sylvia, 1940-
    Kart racing.

    (World of racing)
    Summary: Explains the sport of karting—today's most
important form of big time racing for young people.
    1. Karting—Juvenile literature. [1. Karting]
I. Title. II. Series.
GV1029.5.W54   1985   796.7'6   85-17096
ISBN 0-516-04719-1   AACR2

INTRODUCTION

Karts—or go-karts, as they used to be called—are the smallest motor racing vehicles. At first glance, a kart with driver on board looks like a motorized sled with wheels.

Karts are raced in a variety of ways. In sprint kart racing, the driver sits up as if in a school desk. In road or enduro racing, the driver stretches back as though in a lounge chair. In both classes the racer goes very fast and can have a lot of fun competing across the country and around the world. Kart racing isn't for kids only, yet it is the most important form of big-time racing for young people.

We are going to see how George Mack, a California teenager, got started in kart racing. Then a more experienced and older race driver, Mike Manning, tells the new kart racer how to get ready to go racing.

A 1980 photo of George Mack and his kart being weighed before a race (above). Lloyd Mack uses a battery-connected starter on his son's kart.

GEORGE MACK— KART RACER

When George Mack puts his long legs under the steering wheel of his kart, it is hard to imagine that he was once small for his age. He likes all sports—basketball and football, for example. But already as a teenager, George is sure of the sport he wants to make him famous. He wants to be a professional race car driver.

"All the other sports I play are just for fun. I always try to win, but when I win at racing, I know I have won at the most important thing for me."

George has over a hundred trophies now and has been a kart-class champion four times. But he still remembers vividly being an eleven-year-old rookie racer. Even before his skills had matched his enthusiasm, he knew racing was the sport for him. What does he like most about racing? Nothing complicated. "I just like to go fast," he says with a grin.

George remembers when he saw his first kart race. "My parents and I went to the Queen Mary track in Long Beach," says the California teenager, "just to watch. That was the most exciting sport I had ever seen. I saw them going around and I said to my mom and dad, 'I think I can do that.'"

George's father, Lloyd Mack, was familiar with automobile engines, but karts were a whole new thing for him.

"I stayed up a month of Sundays," he recalled, "reading spec books, trying to learn about the little engines. I knew all the machine shops in the area and had access to good equipment. At first we thought we were just doing it for fun. But pretty soon we knew we were serious. There were times when we almost threw in the towel. It was so hard to make them go fast. People were so competitive that no one would tell me anything. I guess we just had a lot of determination. I said, 'George, let's go beat them.' "

They purchased a membership in IKF, the International Kart Federation, and applied for a number for their kart and a license for George. George likes the number three for his kart. "Three is my lucky number," he says. "Thirty-three is even better because that brings me twice as much luck."

Kart racing for George is a family affair. His dad is still his main mechanic. His mom, Sandra, is his number one fan.

"They were very confident at their first race," Sandra remembers. "They had spent weeks getting ready. They got the kart set up very fast when we got to the track for practice, and nothing went wrong. I kept worrying — maybe it was just beginner's luck. The other drivers told George to follow a certain driver named Peacock around the track and try to keep

George Mack, racing in the reclining position in a road racing (enduro) kart

up with him, that maybe he could learn something. Lloyd and I were watching for the karts to appear and I remember saying 'Lloyd, isn't that George coming down the hill? What in the world is he doing way up there?' George had already passed the driver he was supposed to follow to learn something.''

George recalls that Lee Hatch was the top driver at the time. ''Everyone was afraid of him,'' George says. ''Hatch told me three times to stay out of his way as he went by.''

''George had to start at the back,'' Lloyd adds. ''But by the first lap he was up to twelfth. By the second lap he was in second place.''

The Mack team was off to a roaring start. George knew he was going to be competitive and he knew which driver he had to beat—Lee Hatch.

George and his sister Stephanie (above) hold one of his first karting trophies. By 1982 George (right) was an experienced kart racer.

For George's second race, he went to the track in the harbor parking lot beside the *Queen Mary* where he had first seen karts race. The wind whipped up whitecaps on the ocean, but the sun beamed down on the ocean liner. Even with the wind, it was a perfect day for racing.

Practice went well. George refused to let Hatch crowd him, choosing to race with him in practice instead of moving over for the more experienced racer. Hatch wasn't used to such an attitude.

When asked about intimidation, George replies: "I'll admit I'm nervous when I'm sitting there at the start. I might think about who is in the race, which ones I have to watch out for. I never lose my temper like some guys do and get out and throw

George (#33) takes the lead from Lee Hatch (#6).

my helmet. I'm kind of in a trance when I'm driving, and not thinking about anything else but the race."

"Although all the other drivers had said Hatch was supposed to win," Lloyd said, "George never held back. He could handle the nerves part. Now we had to develop his skills and build him the best kart on the track."

The unexpected happened that day. George Mack won the first heat. Hatch said it was luck, but now people were watching George. In the second heat, Hatch jumped into the lead. George was right behind. It was a tight race, with Hatch leading first, then Mack, then Hatch again. On the last lap George moved just behind Hatch, ready to make his move.

When people are watching a close race between two drivers, they often forget about all the other karts, some several laps behind the front runners but on the same track. As the two fast karts darted through slower traffic, the blue flag went out to a kart in front of them, indicating to the slower racer that he was being overtaken.

The wind caught the flag, so the flagman snatched it flat, startling the slower driver. Unfortunately for George, the driver moved out of Hatch's path and directly in front of George. George let up quickly to keep from driving into the rear of the other kart. By the time he was clear and on the power again, Hatch was too far ahead to catch.

"George was disappointed," Sandra remembers, "but after he had time to think about it, he realized how well he had done. Now everyone knew who he was and he added to his fan club of one!"

In the future George will continue to race karts, looking forward to the day when he can buy his first race car. He wants it to be a Super Vee. He knows it is a dangerous life.

"I'm not scared of breaking bones," George has said, even after his lack of fear was put to the test in two bad accidents. "I'm still not scared of getting hurt. I've done it enough. I broke my collarbone and now both my legs. But that doesn't make me scared of racing. I just learned that when you're going a lot faster, you hit things a lot harder when you mess up.

"When you're racing with a guy, you can't look back. You know he's there. You can hear how close he is. If he gets beside you, you can see him, but you have to keep looking ahead and not give him any chance to get around you. One little mistake and, if he's good, he'll see it and pass you. I was worrying too much about the other drivers and not the track, so I crashed. The worst thing about getting hurt is all the time you're losing when you're waiting to get well and go racing again."

George keeps racing and winning. Today George is racing in the Grand National series for enduro karts. He recently won a race at Willow Springs in California.

In the 1958 kart race at the Eastland Shopping Center Art Ingels was in first place at the turn. Because karts had no bodies, a full-sized adult could fit.

HISTORY OF KARTS

The first kart was built in 1956 by Art Ingels, a hot rodder who built Indy cars in California. The birthplace of the kart was Azusa, California, a town whose name means "everything from A to Z in the USA."

Art got the idea for the first kart while working at Kurtis Kraft in Los Angeles. Kurtis Kraft built quarter midgets, which are small race cars that resemble miniature sprint cars. Often the employees would drive the quarter-midget chassis around the parking lot for fun, leaving the bodies off so a full-size adult would fit.

Art Ingels built the first kart racer in 1956.

In 1960 sports car and sedan champion John Morton raced karts in Tybee, Georgia.

Art Ingels and Lou Borelli designed and built the first six karts in their garages in 1956. Two of those originals are still intact and on display today, one in England and one in the United States. From the beginning the little vehicles were a success, and their popularity has far surpassed the quarter midget.

After World War II, interest in all forms of racing had picked up. Karts were, just as they are today, the most economical way to go racing. And from the time of their invention until now they have served their purpose well: providing a fun, cheap, and safe way to go racing.

At the time the first kart was built, thousands of surplus two-and-one-half horsepower West Bend two-cycle motors

Phil Hill (left) a Grand Prix champion, tried karting. Roberta Moreno
and Nelson Piquet were karting teammates in the 1970s. Piquet,
a Brazilian, later became Formula One World Champion. Moreno races Indy cars.

were available. This came about because a certain McCulloch
lawn mower was withdrawn from the market before the
engine production was stopped. This engine cost only fourteen
dollars. Many early kart components came from other
vehicles: the engines from chain saws and lawn mowers, the
chains from bicycles, and the wheels from hand trucks and
wheelbarrows. Even the original name was borrowed—"go-
karts"—from a brand of baby carriage.

The appeal of karts was instant. They were simple to build.
They were versatile and could be used on all kinds of tracks
that had been built for cars. In fact, all that was needed for an
afternoon of kart racing was an empty parking lot and some
hay bales and pylons to mark the course.

The kart itself had no body, so it could be driven by either
children or adults. It had no suspension. In the rear was a
pedal-operated brake that would stop both rear wheels. In the
front was direct steering and a foot throttle. The engine was

Pit scene at a 1972 kart race in Azusa, California

mounted in the rear and drove one or both wheels. The fuel was a mixture of oil and gas, like the fuel used in two-cycle lawn mowers. Karts were sold in do-it-yourself kit form and became popular as family projects.

Since 1957, the International Kart Federation has published rules for karting and offered its members a varied racing schedule. Rules keep the competition fair and reduce the hazards of the sport. The biggest change in the construction of karts over the years is in the improved quality of the parts. Today the tires, engines, wheels, clutches, and exhaust systems are built especially for karts and do not have to be borrowed from bicycles and mowers. As karts became faster, driver safety became a major consideration. Today drivers are required to wear safety gear: helmets, gloves, jackets, and eye protection.

KARTING TODAY

When karts were first introduced, no one would have believed that someday the little mower engines that power them would be tested on dynos (dynamometers) just like big racing car engines. The dyno, an apparatus that gauges the performance potential of an engine, is used to get peak power from a racing engine. As karters become better drivers, they demand that engines produce more power, leading them to rely on professional engine builders.

Such a builder is Mike Manning, a national champion driver himself, who runs his own business—Mike Manning Karting.

Mike Manning's 1982 Speedway Grandnational Champion in the super/stock class.

Mike experiments with new exhaust pipes and new engine settings, using an engine on the dyno in his shop. He explains, "All of the fastest drivers have dynoed engines, but the dyno is still not the ultimate test facility. The race track is. I always use the track to verify what I discover on the dyno."

As a driver becomes more competitive, the cost of racing goes up. The kart needs new tires more often to go that extra tenth of a second faster. The driver wants his engine to be freshly rebuilt (or "fresher") and he must buy the latest developments in equipment. A beginning karter can get more races out of a set of tires and an engine than an advanced karter can. This is because the beginner has not reached a level of excellence yet to demand the ultimate in equipment.

Mike Manning sees karting as a good way to prepare to be a race car driver. "I think it is great for kids to get started in karting if they think they want to become a race car driver someday. It is the only real form of racing where they can start at the age of eight. Our reflexes are at their maximum when we are young, and we have no fears to cope with. You can get eight years of racing experience behind you before you are sixteen, the age that you are allowed to start in any other form of racing. Karting teaches you to drive with finesse—with your fingers, not your foot."

Manning, the 1980 Sprint Grandnational Champion, races here in the 100cc stock heavy class.

On the other hand, Mike reasons, karting does not give the young racer a true picture of the costs of other forms of racing. "The prices are great for the sport of karting, but it leads some young racers to live in a dream world. He can buy a brand-new high-quality kart for only $1,500 to $2,000, while his first race car in used condition will cost ten times that."

GETTING STARTED

The biggest expense for a kart racer is the kart itself. It can be transported to the race track in any number of ways: in a van, in a small pickup truck, on a trailer, even on the roof or in the trunk of the family car.

After the purchase of a kart, the main operating expense will be engine rebuilds and new tires. While just learning, a racer can delay buying new tires or getting the engine rebuilt until competitive racing begins.

Besides purchasing the kart, a racer must buy a starter. The starter, which can come from an automobile or motorcycle, is not carried on board the kart. It is connected to a storage battery, and someone other than the driver uses it to start the kart.

George Mack wears a padded leather suit and a helmet for protection.

The kart racer also must purchase some personal safety equipment. The minimum are a jacket, gloves, and an approved helmet with ear and eye protection. The jacket, which should be of heavyweight vinyl, nylon, or leather, protects the karter when turning over or being thrown off the kart. Many karters wear full leather suits and boots that protect the whole body. Certain closed-body road-racing karts called Formula Kart Experimental require the driver to wear Nomex or fire-resistant clothing. Earplugs are recommended to protect the hearing. Each racer must have a fire extinguisher handy.

21

Preparing the Kart

Before leaving for the track, the kart racer checks to see if all the equipment needed to prepare the kart for racing is handy. For instance, every racer needs a small toolbox with a carefully selected collection of tools that fit all the nuts and bolts on the kart. Other essential items are chain lube, a five-gallon container of the gas-oil mixture to run the engine, a drip pan, a selection of spark plugs, a tire pump or air tank, and a starter with battery.

Before going to the track, the karter should give the kart a safety inspection. At an organized event the kart must pass a safety inspection, but when you are just out for a practice

Kart and the equipment needed to race

Karts are carefully checked and rechecked before every race. A kart is placed on a stand so you can work on it without bending over.

session you must be your own inspector. Because of vibrations, tight nuts can loosen and should be constantly rechecked.

"Make sure all your bolts are cotter keyed," Mike says. "Inspect your wheels, check your tire pressures, your fuel lines, the chain guards. You would be surprised how many times that, due to carelessness, accidents happen because wheels fall off or the steering comes undone.

"Also it is very important to clean the spark plug often on a one-cylinder engine. Good maintenance means you catch problems before they begin, and all your time at the track can be concentrated on improving your driving and setting up your kart."

George and his dad, Lloyd Mack, weigh their kart.

Weighing In

After each qualifying event, the racer must roll the kart directly to the scales before returning to the pit area and before a mechanic touches the kart. Kart and driver are weighed together. This rule is enforced strictly to keep the racing fair.

When you get to the track, you should weigh yourself with your kart. In the week between races it is possible to gain a pound because many karters are young and still growing. You are allowed to take that one pound off your kart. Because scales may vary, weight should be checked at each race track.

If you and your kart are too light, you can add weight by bolting lead to the kart. You can also put lead shot inside the suspension or in a container that is firmly attached to the kart.

DRIVING SKILLS

Mike Manning has a word of caution for the beginning driver. "A kart is not a toy. It is a real racing vehicle that is capable of very high speeds. Most young racers are too young to drive cars on the public roads, so they haven't experienced the kinds of speeds they will feel their first time in a kart. I suggest that they start at half-speed until they learn the limits. The speeds on the straights can be very thrilling. Then you find you can't make it through the corner. For a while, a young driver will experience lots of spinouts."

When young racers begin to drive quickly with other karts around them, Mike says they need to learn how to move through traffic. "It is important from a safety standpoint to remember they are open-wheeled vehicles. If you hit another kart's wheel, you can tip over. If you leave the track and run over something such as a corner marker or rock, you can also tip over."

Kim Williams fine tunes his carburetor.

It is possible for a driver to adjust the carburetor while racing. To do this, the driver can reach back while on the straight part of the course and turn a screw. The two fuel characteristics are lean and rich. The engine must run lean enough to obtain maximum power. This means the carburetor is set for a smaller (or leaner) amount of fuel. If it is set too rich, it is set for too much fuel and will falter during acceleration. If the driver turns the screw too far toward lean, the engine can overheat and lose power.

Young racers must learn how to adjust their engines while moving their karts through heavy traffic.

"It is important to remember," Mike Manning cautions, "that 'too rich' will not hurt your engine, but 'too lean' will. Don't just start turning the screw because you see the fast drivers doing it. Also, don't lose your driving concentration while fiddling with your engine. Practice, practice, practice. Step up to new and better equipment and start doing fine tuning when *you* get better as a driver. Don't just try to buy things to make you better. You are the most important item on your kart."

KART CLASSES

Chris Smith, son of well-known auto-racing mechanic Carroll Smith, remembers how his father first got him interested in karting.

"My dad talks about racing all the time. One day he was talking to some racers and I heard them mention karts and that you didn't have to be an adult to drive. I kept bringing it up until he said we could try it. He had no experience with karts, but he related what he knew about cars. Now we do all of our own preparation except the motor work.

"Actually I don't have time to play other sports because the kart takes up almost all of my free time. Someday I want to race Formula Fords. Right now, this is the only kind of racing that I am old enough to do, and I think it will give me a lot of the experience I need to be a racing driver. Karts teach you car control and the feeling of being in very close competition with other drivers."

Chris Smith

Chris suggests that a young person interested in kart racing should go to many different kinds of kart races to see which one is most appealing. Chris prefers sprint karts to road racing karts, for example, because he feels they do a better job of training him for future racing. George Mack, on the other hand, likes the road racing kart best because of the high speeds. Let's take a look at the different classes available: 4-cycle, sprint, speedway, and road racing.

4-Cycle

The 4-cycle class is often a youngster's first racing experience. The 4-cycle uses the same chassis as the faster 2-cycle engine class. The use of the stock 4-cycle five-horsepower lawn mower engine makes this a popular class for very young racers. They can start as young as eight years old in the Rookie Junior group. The stock engine keeps racing costs to a minimum. Because the horsepower is so low, kart owners use narrower tires and pay close attention to any part that might cause friction and slow them down. There are many races for this group. A serious racer has the opportunity to compete up to three times a month without traveling far from home.

Ten-year-old Nate Arrison races his 4-cycle kart at Rattlesnake Mountain Speedway in Winchester, New Hampshire.

Sprint

For the next step up, the young racer can advance to a sprint kart by replacing his 4-cycle stock engine with a 2-cycle racing engine. Sprint karts are the oldest form of racing kart. They are recognizable by their "sit-up" driving position. Sprint karts race on miniature road courses that are generally one-quarter to one-half mile in length. These courses have a variety of turns, some very slow and some very fast.

One sprint race event is usually broken down into three heats, each eight to ten laps long. A sprint kart races at speeds up to sixty or seventy miles per hour, about half the speed of a road racing kart. Drivers for these karts—as well as for the speedway karts, discussed next—can be as young as nine years old.

Most sprint events have open practice, a time when all the classes can set up their karts and run them. After practice are time trials, which consist of a warm-up lap and two timed laps. This sets the order in which the drivers will start the first heat. The starting order for each consecutive heat is determined by the finishing order of the preceding heat. The overall winner is determined by combining the finishes from all three heats.

Sprint karts race at Quincy, Illinois

Chris Smith gives his opinion on sprint kart racing: "If you want to be a road racing driver some day in full-size race cars, I think that sprint karts give you more experience than road racing karts. Although with the road racing kart you would be running on the same tracks as you would with a race car, a kart is too easy to drive flat out on a road racing track. On a sprint track you have to learn to brake for corners. I think that the braking and cornering give you more practice at the kind of racing you will need if you step up to cars."

Speedway

For a young driver eager to get in the most racing time for the least amount of money, speedway karting has great appeal. The same sit-up style sprint kart is used, but with a different type of tire, since a speedway track has a dirt surface. The cost of karting can be kept down because tires last longer racing on dirt than on pavement. Since they need more grip on the loose dirt surface, the tires have a grooved or treaded surface instead of the slick surface used on pavement.

Dirt track racing is an American form of racing that started early in this century on horse tracks at fairgrounds. Speedway karting caught on because of the availability of quarter-mile race tracks that were already built for sprint cars and stock cars, which are often run on oval or circle dirt tracks.

Workers prepare the dirt track at Saddleback Park.

Pits at Saddleback (left) and close-up of a dirt kart (right). Note the treaded tires.

A typical race event has two ten-lap heats and one twenty-lap heat. Chris Smith finds speedway racing even closer than sprint racing. "The tracks are wide so it is easier to pass, but the racing is closer and it takes more physical stamina to drive on dirt. If you get your kart set up right and drive well, you can be a little down on horsepower and still beat the guy with the stronger engine. If your engine is getting too tired to race on a sprint track, but you don't have the money to get it rebuilt right then, you can put on the dirt tires and go speedway racing."

Speedway karts are exciting to watch "broadsliding" through turns, a car-racing technique used in sprint car racing. To broadslide, the driver pitches the kart sideways and slides through the turn with foot on the throttle.

Racers (above) wait for the signal to start their engines.
Sprint or sit-up karts are sometimes raced on road courses.

Road Racing

Road racing karts, or enduro karts, are raced on full-sized, paved, road racing tracks used for sports car and Indy car racing, such as Riverside and Road America. They also race on courses in other countries, such as Silverstone in England and Le Mans in France. Road races are much longer, usually one hour. The driving position is different from the sprint or speedway kart position. Also, the costs for this type of kart racing are higher.

At first the road racing kart driver sat up straight and used a sprint-type kart. It was soon discovered that aerodynamics — the effect of air on a moving object — was improved if the driver sat in a horizontal rather than vertical position.

"The karts were developed," Mike Manning explains, "by laying the driver down in much the same position he would take in an enclosed sports car. This cuts down on wind resistance. Also, the chassis of the kart had to be lengthened to achieve this position."

Single-engine road racing karts go up to 124 miles per hour. Karts with larger engines or dual engines go as high as 140 miles per hour. The road racing kart has bodywork added to it

High-speed enduro karts are growing in popularity in the United States.

that, in addition to the laydown position, reduces wind resistance. The karts also have larger, side-mounted, fuel tanks because road races are longer.

George Mack, who broke his legs at Laguna Seca Raceway while racing an enduro kart, says: "I like racing enduro karts because they go faster and the tracks are longer. But you can't afford to spin out. Once you start to go out of control, you can't stop the kart. It's like you are on ice. Smoke comes off your tires, and you spin so fast you don't have time to think. You have to work on your technique and drive tight and clean. On

dirt in the speedway races, your style is completely different. You have to drive rougher, pitch the kart sideways, and keep it sideways through the turns. It's fun, but you don't have to learn to be as careful."

A very-high-speed enduro kart, very popular in Europe and growing more popular in the United States, is called the Super Kart. Mike Manning hopes these will not catch on in the U.S. because they are too dangerous. "The speeds they reach are much too high for a kart. After all, the purpose of kart racing is close competition. Those high speeds should be left to racing cars that have full roll bars and cages to protect the drivers."

A 4-cycle sprint kart race (above) at the Atwater
track. John Morton, the consultant for this
book, still owns and races a kart (below).

CONCLUSION

Some people think racing karts sound like a swarm of hornets. Or an army of chain saws and lawn mowers. Yet many famous racing people can trace their first excitement over racing to the sounds the racers make. Racing beauty queen Linda Vaughn heard stock cars on a dirt track, climbed the fence to see them, and got a spanking for coming home with red clay on her feet. Sports car champion Dan Gurney was in the family car when he first heard cars on a road course in Long Island, New York, but couldn't get his dad to stop.

Drivers all over the world can remember their earliest racing experiences as children and how thrilling it was to hear the sound of their kart engines and feel the speed. Most of the famous drivers started on karts. World champions Niki Lauda, Emerson Fittipaldi, Nelson Piquet, Alan Jones, Jody Scheckter, and Keke Rosberg all raced karts. So did stock car champion Darrell Waltrip and sports car champion Al Holbert. Al Unser, Jr., went from karts to Indianapolis in only six years.

Don Lierle, father of champion kart racer Doug Lierle, describes a memory familiar to many of today's participants: "We heard them and went and looked and we've been involved ever since."

41

Kart racers prepare for their next heat.

For additional information on karting, contact: International Kart Federation, 416 South Grand, Covina, California 91724. Phone (213) 967-4197.

Glossary

aerodynamics: the branch of dynamics that deals with the force of air on a moving object such as a racing kart

amateur racing: racing competition for personal pleasure with trophies as the prize but no money

apex: the point in a corner where the kart comes closest to the inside of the road, where corner entry ends and exit begins

back marker: a kart driver running near the back of the pack in the last rows of the grid

back off: let off the throttle, slow down

bicycle: to get a four-wheel vehicle up on two wheels

bore: the diameter of a cylinder (*see* cylinder)

broadsliding: dirt-track driving technique in which the kart is thrown sideways to slow its forward motion enough to negotiate a turn

carburetor: an apparatus on an internal combustion engine that mixes fuel with air, sending it into the combustion chamber in vapor form by suction from the piston

chain: the device that transmits engine power from the crankshaft to the rear axle by linking the clutch and axle sprockets

chicane: an artificial turn consisting of speed bumps or barriers placed on a fast section of a road-racing track to slow the karts

clutch: the controllable link used to engage or disengage the engine from the rest of the drive train

combustion: the process of igniting fuel in a chamber to produce power. The engine that works in this manner is called an *internal combustion engine.*

corkscrew turn: a very tight turn that winds in the shape of a corkscrew

cornering: the act of driving through a turn

cotter key cotter pin: a metal strip bent double into a pin whose ends can be flared after insertion through a slot or hole

cushion: the soft dirt area at the top of the track, formed when karts toss up loose dirt

cylinder: a chamber in an internal combustion engine through which a piston moves driven by the combustion process

decreasing radius turn: a very difficult turn that gets tighter as the car travels through and must be exited slower than it was entered

designer: a person who creates a kart in blueprint (drawing) form

dicing: close, highly competitive racing between two or more karts

dogleg, kink: a slight bend in the road of short duration, usually taken at high speed

downforce: (also called download) the desirable force produced by air passing over and under a moving kart that presses the kart to the ground

drag: a retarding aerodynamic force on a moving body, parallel and opposite to the direction of motion

dyno, dynamometer: an apparatus usually placed in a soundproof chamber, used to measure the performance capabilities of an engine before it is installed in a kart. Also used as a verb: He dynoed the engine.

endurance race: a competition that requires both speed and the ability to last or endure

enduro or road racing kart: a small racing vehicle used on longer road racing circuits built for race cars, featuring a horizontal driving position, one-hour races, and speeds in excess of 125 mph

engine displacement: the size of an engine, measured in cubic inches (ci, cu. ins.), cubic centimeters (cc.), cubin inch displacement (CID, c.i.d.), or liters, not including combustion chamber size

envelope body: a body on a racing kart that offers no structural support. It covers the chassis, the working parts, and the wheels with a cockpit opening and various small openings to admit air to the areas that need cooling (brakes, radiators, exhaust)

esses: a continuous series of left and right turns on a road course, like the letter "S"

fabricator: a highly skilled metalworker who builds new structures (such as prototypes) or improves existing structures

fiberglass: glass in a bendable fiber form. When the glass is combined with resin and a catalyst (a substance used to cause a chemical reaction), it becomes fiberglass, a hard, lightweight substance used for kart bodies

flags: internationally recognized signal system used in racing, displayed beside the track by flagmen and/or corner workers

flat-out: full throttle

flip: to turn a kart over

four-cycle, four-stroke engine: an internal combustion engine that performs intake, compression, power, and exhaust with four strokes (i.e., up/down, up/down) of the piston

four-cycle kart: a kart that utilizes a four-cycle, five-horsepower engine, frequently raced by younger drivers; the oldest type of kart

get sideways: go into a slide that puts the kart at an angle to the direction of traffic

grid: the starting positions of karts in a race as determined by qualifying. Also, the place on the track where karts are brought to prior to the start of a race. Examples: He is third on the grid. Show me a grid sheet. His kart is gridded third. Bring the karts to the grid.

guardrail: a metal barrier around a road race track

hairpin: a tight turn in the shape of a hairpin

handling: the kart's reaction to the manual controls, i.e., braking, accelerating, steering

headers: the part of the exhaust system that attaches to the cylinder heads to carry off burned gases from the engine, a performance improvement which replaces the more restrictive exhaust manifold

helmet: protective head covering consisting of a hard shell with foam liner and chin strap

horsepower: standard unit of power used to measure engine output, equal to 746 watts and 550 foot-pounds of work per second

hot-lapping: high speed practice on a fresh track

IKF: International Kart Federation; the organization that governs kart racing in the U.S.

increasing radius turn: a turn that opens up and can be exited faster than it was entered

independent suspension: a suspension system that isolates each wheel (*see* solid axle)

Indy car: a high-powered, single-seat, open-cockpit, and open-wheel car used in North American competition, on oval tracks such as Indianapolis and Pocono, and on road-racing tracks such as Road America

kart, go-kart: the smallest racing vehicle made, consisting of a seat, a frame, four tiny wheels, a motor (usually two-cycle), and simple brake, clutch, and chain-driven axle

lap: a complete circuit of a race course

lean: engine condition, set for too little fuel to be used. A lean engine will lose power and can damage a piston from excessive heat (*see* rich).

lose it: lose control of a kart

manifold: a chamber that (1) takes the fuel-air mixture from the carburetor to the cylinder head (intake manifold) or (2) takes the exhaust to the exhaust pipes (exhaust manifold)

midget: a race car very much like a sprint car but smaller, with about one-third the power

mount: to assemble a tire and wheel

Nomex: trademark, a fire-resistant fabric used in driver's clothing

open-wheeled: without fenders

oval: an oval-shaped race track

pace lap: a lap taken by the competitors before the start of a race to warm up the karts and to prepare for a moving or flying start

piston: a hollow cylindrically-shaped piece of aluminum with a solid top (or crown) that is attached to a connecting rod by a pin (called a wrist pin). A piston travels back and forth inside a cylinder in an internal combustion engine.

pit (noun), pitted (verb): the area beside the race track, usually on a straightaway, that is used for refueling and servicing the karts

pit pass: a pass given to competitors and crew at an auto race that allows them to go into the working pit area where spectators aren't allowed

plug: short for spark plug, a device that fits into the cylinder head of an internal combustion engine and provides the spark to ignite the fuel (*see* combustion)

pole position: the number-one qualifier, the inside position

qualifying: an on-track session where drivers demonstrate their speed in relation to other kart/driver combinations, determining their starting positions and/or whether they can reach the speed required to run the race

quarter midget: a miniature midget raced by very young drivers, usually pre-teenagers; uses basically modified lawn mower engine

rich: engine condition, set for too much fuel to be used. A rich engine falters during acceleration, and also lacks maximum potential power.

road racing: a form of racing that takes place on closed circuit tracks (in the U.S., from 1.5 to 5.2 miles long), designed to resemble a country road with a variety of turns and hills

roll bar: a metal hoop in a race car to protect the driver in a turnover

rookie: a driver in his or her first season of racing

solid axle: a single axle used by both left and right wheels, as a wagon axle (opposite of independent)

speedway kart: a sprint-racing kart used on dirt or speedway tracks with treaded tires (*see* sprint kart)

spin: to go out of control and revolve. A driver can "spin out" and stay on course, or "spin off" the track.

sprint car: a sturdy, high-powered, open-wheel, usually front-engine race car with roll cage, raced on dirt tracks used by speedway karts

sprint kart: a small racing vehicle with slick tires, with the driver in a sit-up position in front of or beside the two-cycle engine; used on miniature road course tracks, usually one-quarter to one-half mile in length

sprocket: a disc with teeth on its perimeter that engages a chain to transmit drive from one sprocket to another. The number of teeth on the sprocket pairs forms a ratio which governs engine speed to wheel speed.

stick: adhesion. Examples: The tires are sticking well. The car was sticking well in the rear. *Bite* means traction coming off a turn. Example: The rear wheels were getting more bite.

straight, straightaway: the part of a race track that travels in a straight line; therefore, the fastest part of the track

stroke: distance the piston travels in the cylinder

super kart: a more powerful road racing kart, first popularized in Europe, featuring gear boxes, often four-wheel brakes and water-cooled engines, and a driving position between sit-up and lay-down

Super Vee: a small, approx. 950-pound, open-wheel, single-seat, rear-engined race car using the VW Rabbit engine and many VW parts, raced in a professional series that attracts young drivers

technical, tech inspection: an inspection of a kart to determine if it is safe and if it conforms to the rules

three-quarter midget: slightly smaller than a midget, usually powered by a large motorcycle engine

tread: the pattern of slots, grooves, and ridges on the surface of a tire

two-cycle engine: an internal combustion engine that performs intake, compression, power, and exhaust with two strokes of the piston, up and down

valve: a mechanical device used to temporarily close a passage and/or to permit flow in one direction only of a liquid and/or gas

visor: clear or tinted plastic eye protection that attaches to a helmet

Index

About the Author
Sylvia Wilkinson was born in Durham, North Carolina and studied at the University of North Carolina, Hollins College, and Stanford University. She has taught at UNC, William and Mary, Sweet Briar, and Washington University, and is currently Associate Professor of English at the University of Wisconsin-Milwaukee and a consultant for the National Humanities Faculty. Her awards include a Eugene Saxton Memorial Trust Grant, a Wallace Stegner Creative Writing Fellowship, a *Mademoiselle* Merit Award for Literature, two Sir Walter Raleigh Awards for fiction, a National Endowment for the Arts grant and a Guggenheim fellowship. In addition to five novels, she has written two nonfiction books on auto racing, *The Stainless Steel Carrot* and *Dirt Tracks to Glory;* an adventure series on auto racing; an education handbook; and articles for *Sports Illustrated, Mademoiselle, Ingenue, True, The American Scholar, The Writer,* and others; and is currently a contributing editor for *Autoweek.*

Sylvia Wilkinson is timer and scorer for Bobby Rahal's Truesports Indy racing team, for IMSA GTU Champion Jack Baldwin, and for the Nissan prototype.